HIS pageturner

HIS pageturner

John E. Heim

RESOURCE *Publications* · Eugene, Oregon

HIS PAGETURNER

Resource Publications
An Imprint of Wipf and Stock Publishers
199 W. 8th Ave., Suite 3
Eugene, OR 97401

www.wipfandstock.com

PAPERBACK ISBN: 979-8-3852-4590-1
HARDCOVER ISBN: 979-8-3852-4591-8
EBOOK ISBN: 979-8-3852-4592-5

VERSION NUMBER 04/14/25

In moments like these I sing out a song,
I sing out a love song to Jesus.
In moments like these I lift up my hands,
I lift up my hands to the Lord.
Singing I love You, Lord.
Singing I love You, Lord.
Singing I love You, Lord,
I love You.

CONTENTS

INTRODUCTION

In the King James Version of the Bible, in a section known as the New Testament, there appears a letter written by the Apostle Paul in the year 55-56 AD, from Macedonia to the church that resided in Corinth, located in Greece, being a region above the Aegean and Ionian Seas. History tells us that Paul had written his first letter to the church approximately one year prior to what is now commonly known as the book or letter of Second Corinthians. On his second missionary journey after his visit to Athens in Greece in the years 50-51 AD, he stayed with Aquilla and Pricilla in Corinth, after having been expelled from Rome. While there, staying for approximately eighteen months, he established a community of believers in Jesus Christ and worked as a tent maker for his living. Corinth was a very liberal and wicked city of much immorality and fleshly customs.

Teaching the scriptures of the Word of God caused him to be persecuted and reviled because he spoke often of the things prompted by the Holy Spirit, who guided and counseled Paul to begin his times in the church there to be more than what was visible before the eyes of those who would eventually come to understand what Paul was teaching about the Holy Ghost and the Trinity. In the bible today and as it was translated in 1611 under the order of King James, chapters and verses were assigned to the text of each book or letter, now referred to as epistles written by Paul. In the

Second Letter or Epistle to the Corinthians, in the fourth chapter, he writes this verse found at the bottom of the chapter.

> *While we look not at the things which are seen, but at the things which are not seen: for the things which are seen are temporal; but the things which are not seen are eternal.*

In the previous seventeen verses of chapter four, Paul, though being tormented and tested, along with the congregation, while living amongst the most vile and vulgar of people, is prompted to tell them that what is now happening on a daily basis in everyday life is nothing compared to the eons of time spent seeing things of eternity that are called the unseen or not seen. To live by the power of the Holy Spirit and endure daily trials and tribulations for the sake of the Gospel is to live as Christ and therefore obtain eternal rewards.

As Paul experienced the delight of seeing the church of Corinth prosper and grow in things that were not seen but only by the power given from above and then manifested into the lives of the believer, I present to you the exact same power only given by the Holy Spirit, which I truly believe most people today have never experienced but has been available to many for all the years you have known and trusted Jesus as your Savior. In this book or resource that you have chosen, to perhaps, explore the many discussions you have had with yourself, about the topic of the unseen, I hope sincerely that you will find what is missing from your time with Jesus. To clarify that statement and to expand the idea of a missing part to your walk by faith is not to say that you are lacking at all. But you know why you are asking for something that you want desperately but are not sure that you are really missing anything that is and always has been available. In this work that has come expressly from the heart of your wonderful, ever-present and all-knowing God; you will find what you are seeking. But, please remember this most important aspect of the whole reason you are looking into the unseen; it is not mystical or bizarre, not other world or outer space type of the unseen, it is scriptural and divinely inspired.

> *Second Timothy chapter 3:16*
>
> *All scripture is given by inspiration of God, and is profitable for doctrine, for reproof, for correction, for instruction in righteousness: That the man of God may be perfect, thoroughly furnished unto all good works.*

This simple, yet hopefully revealing piece of literature, does not attempt to add or take away from anything of the inspired Word of God. The author chooses to make note of the fact that the original idea of the topic given and then spoken into his heart, is solely credited to the work of the Holy Spirit. When the narrator of this book is spoken about, it is to give all glory and honor to the One who has asked it to be written. Therefore, please treat this as something that you would always point to God as helping you understand the true meaning of covenant relationship. While we now live together in a temporal world, let us place our hope entirely in the eternal; the unseen but certainly not the hidden. Blessings!

CHAPTER 1

IN MOMENTS LIKE THESE

I KNEW THE DAY would come that it would have to be done. All the preparations had been made, but the reality of the moment seemed to bring to mind nothing but the thought of indecision. I could watch him begin to slip further into the state of helplessness and see in his eyes those questions of why this was happening to him. As the time drew near for the veterinarian to arrive at the door as planned, I pulled him on his blanket from the foyer to the garage where she would administer the shots that would end his pain and suffering that none of us in the household could allow to go on for one more day.

Our second yellow labrador retriever we named Paulie, after the apostle Paul, because our first yellow lab was named Barnabas, chosen from a book that we loved about a pastor and his wife and their wonderful big dog named Barnabas. Of course, we knew that the two would be companions as was written in the book of acts in the bible. When Barnabas was put to sleep at the age of fifteen, Paulie was about five. I thought that the world had ended the day I drove Barnabas to the vet to be put to sleep. He was my friend and constant sidekick and really didn't like another male hanging around me so they were somewhat distant because

Barnabas did not want Paulie to be affectionate to me and being the alpha, he let him know that.

When Paulie was then the only dog we had, I was unaware of the difference in the two at first. I soon found out that Paulie was naturally capable on learning just about anything that I asked of him. The breeding of the two was similar but the field expertise of Paulie was so evident. Commands and hand signals became common language to him and he loved doing whatever I asked. You might have guessed what was coming next. He made me almost forget the wonderful relationship I had with Barnabas and he became so loving to all of us that he soon found his way into our hearts without much coaxing.

We are fortunate to have a home here on these 1.2 acres of fenced land with a house that we built ourselves providing a perfect surrounding for the two dogs and plenty of landscaping and trees that made it quite enjoyable and pleasant to spend hour after hour with each other. As the author of this book, now as a retired engineering kind of guy and living with my wife of 56 years and our adult daughter also, we have had so many memories as I am sure you have also.

Now is the time that we must face the section of the book that will deal solely with the unseen. I knew it was there and knew that it had purpose but I am sure that the expectation of the moment was anything but one of reality. It could be to you a completely different subject matter and one that I may have never imagined and certainly did not invite to be now my companion and constant reminder.

I ventured down to my chair in the great room where every night I would end my day with a reading of the proverbs of that day and if it where fall or winter, the fireplace most likely would be burning. The time was perfect because Paulie was always right there . . . but not that night. My wife and daughter were upstairs and I would then leave them and be alone with the Lord and my friend. You may already be in that state of being alone and single or lonesome and, although you have the time to sit and read and pray, as is often the case, comfort does not come. You have lost someone or something and now it is up to you alone to make the day, that would lead into the week, month and year and then years, and you are not feeling the presence of Jesus that you supposed it would be. After all, is not the promise of God that He would never leave you to forsake you and that He would give you the peace that passes all understanding? What might be the problem with my relationship with God?

That night, sitting alone and feeling the absence of a friend that was only an animal yet more than that, I began to ask God for His presence which was not a new idea and because He had so faithfully given my daughter the ability to let her friend go that afternoon and be without him then and now forever, I had nothing but praise and worship for Him. The reality of the God I had invited into my life almost exactly forty-five years ago, proved to be another amazing event that night. Finishing the reading of the twenty-third proverb, being October the twenty-third, and then desiring to stay by the fire and pray, I found myself unable to do so. It would have been one of thanksgiving and praise, but a strong sense of this hand upon me caused me to listen with the heart that He gave me to do just that; listen! In moments like these, there is a distinct awareness of something new being done that maybe the loss and being alone caused the familiar to escape and the unseen appear. If that is something that you may have noticed in times past, as you find that the words you wanted to speak out of your heart to the Shephard of your soul, did not materialize as you would have remembered Them to do, but now only silence and a peace that truly does pass your understanding.

This manuscript is being born out of such a moment. As the scripture in the beginning of our time together stated in the introduction and proclaimed, this occasion for silence and listening is apparently not of the temporal at all, but that of an eternal, heavenly epoch known to us as the unseen. But we ask ourselves at the time and now as we are being instructed by the narrator of this piece of literature, our Holy Spirit of God; why did it feel that something now made real to us, seems as it had been there all the while yet, up until a moment like this, it was missing from our lives as believers.

Purposes of things that have never been experienced before, seem to surprise us when in actuality, they should be expectations that drive us nearer to the Giver. What is meant by that is explained to us in scripture as we see that written in Second Corinthians 5:17 "Therefore, if any man be in Christ, he is a new creature: old things are passed away; behold, all things are become new."

To sit alone in a chair near the fireplace with a feeling of need to talk to God in prayer is an exceptional, rather miraculous, divinely appointed moment. What has passed away from us was meant to die, permanently and forever; that being the flesh. But. Most unfortunately, the new creature born again in Jesus Christ, is often left to believe that what is true and eternal does not always apply to all of our daily lives. This is where the concept of missing something is brought to bear. If all that you and I read in the word of God and we seem to bear witness of the truth that is embedded within it, why is that a wonderment of heart and mind in actually believing that whatever is spoken or thought and even groaned as the word says, may not at all reach the One we are making conversation with? In other words, I hear you but am I really listening and reacting to what it is You are desperately needing me to know? Sharing this with you makes little sense if I, as the author, and or you as the reader, do not fully believe by faith in God, that Jesus, the Holy Spirit, and the Father truly occupy the very place and thoughts directed toward them by us, *in moments like these!*

Let's go on now into an essential matter that may sound familiar but just might open up into a place of new beginnings. The Holy Spirit is our guide into wherever we will venture that is the will of God. Jesus was a man on this earth that if you are following Jesus Christ, you'll probably find yourself doing things you swore you'd never do, because there was never a more inconsistent being on this earth than our Lord. But He was never inconsistent to His Father. The one consistency of the disciple is loyalty not to a conviction or a principle but to the divine life. When you were called and chosen by God, and that being from the foundation of the world, by the way, you were then created to be like the Son of God as He was on this earth. Our example is one person and one only. So many wonderful books and pieces of fine writings have been published and many that were written never made it to print. Remember the part about Jesus and His Father. Although we have desires within us to be as Jesus was with His Father, ours is and can be considered those things that are menial and a waste of time; but not to the Father.

So, how can I know that I am doing the will of the Father and not just acting out a form of piety or duty that I have believed for many years, as being the relationship with God that I want and treasure but something is missing and certainly not satisfying to my spiritual self!? The scriptures that have been shared previously have dealt with that of a divine nature and one that is misunderstood and mostly has become unwelcome territory to the average believer. In the work a day world that we are all a part of and must dwell in it from birth to death. Mathematics is used thousands of times a day in each individuals life and millions upon millions of times we just plain disregard the idea that the hours in one day are given to each and every person that is alive on this earth and each person is then given the freedom to use those hours as he or she wishes. Much could be added to this fact but I will not be the one who does that. We have a subject matter to get to and the narrator is tapping me on the shoulder and reminding me that there is a schedule to keep. Those scriptures in the introduction and in second Corinthians five seventeen, all have a common thread running through them, that being man and God. Simply put and often overlooked in the world we are a part of today and in all of history; there is no way to separate the two. Incredibly, God has chosen man from the beginning, to be a vital part of Himself! What did you just say? Yes, that is right. God is crazy about you. He never takes His mind off of you and that means you! Personally, and intimately. We are saying here that all of God's chosen and called and predestined, are so precious and valuable to Him that His plan is for eternity, the unseen, is to last forever; together.

I am sure that not everyone who may be reading this book is born again. Many are leaning toward the religious side of a relationship with God, some have a Christian background from a

Godly mother or grandfather and even a neighbor. Most of the world is worshipping gods by the millions and living as if that will provide heavenly rewards. To ask them about these things would be to receive back just about any response that can be imagined. Yet, all would say that the life they are now living is the one they want whether they are happy and content in it or miserable and tormented each day with the lack of peace of mind and no hope. That is the world we live in from our birth to our death. Certainly, gods come in all shapes and sizes and to many in the world today, self is the only one that matters and to expect anything of a God who no one has ever seen and then base your entire, say 77 years of life, on faith in an unseen God is ridiculous and that is not going to happen. So, what about you? What does the title of this book say to you? After reading the first few pages, have you decided that it is not something you want to read and be talked about spiritual matters and nearness to God or can you believe that the Holy Spirit is right here with us and something that is missing is about to be unveiled and retrieved? We will see.

CHAPTER 2

I SING OUT A SONG

> Redeeming the time, because the days are evil. Wherefore be ye not unwise, but understanding what the will of the Lord is. And be not drunk with wine, wherein is excess; but be filled with the Spirit; *speaking to yourselves in psalms and hymns and spiritual songs, singing and making melody in your heart to the Lord;* giving thanks always for all things unto God and the Father in the name of our Lord Jesus Christ.

THE WORDS WRITTEN IN italics and those surrounding it, are given to Paul in the book of Ephesians chapter five by the Holy Spirit. Verse nineteen includes action words that would confuse most who would consider the command here to be somewhat unusual if not a cause to question the mentality of the writer and also those he is communicating with in Ephesus and now also, you the reader. Searching for a reason to believe that something just might be missing from our relationship with Jesus, His Father and the Holy Spirit, the very best and most honoring of all places to begin that journey is to go directly to the Word of God.

The title of this chapter, I SING OUT A SONG, gives us an all-important hint into the discovery of our question. As the author, inspired by the narrator, I may be the writer of this text, like Paul is the author and writer of Ephesians, but I also, along with you, the reader, have begun to understand the completeness of what relationship actually mean. Is ours to be as a friend only with the Three in One or is it as an acquaintance would be, or more intimate as a family member? Just what is it to look like and why the necessity to know for sure that I honestly have a relationship at all? Would we all want that relationship to be one of love? Boy, if we are to ever understand the meaning of that word, there has to be a whole lot of transparency happening; one that deals with the heart and one that does not allow for anything other than truth. Dear reader, you have now brought into your being something that is not optional or able to be considered in part but not whole. In other words, are you sure that you want to proceed into a realm of the spiritual known as the unseen and embrace it to the point to a complete overhaul of heart and mind? Who is the One identified in the book of Isaiah chapter 9:6 *For unto us a child is born, unto us a Son is given: and the government shall be upon His shoulder: and His name shall be called wonderful, counselor, the mighty God, the everlasting Father, the prince of peace.*

This One, who is absolutely born to be a governor that shoulders the entire responsibility of guiding man in the way of righteousness, has a name that, although not given here, is assumed to be unlike any other name ever spoken. Wouldn't you think that with that surety of promise from the prophet, received by the Holy Spirit, and now distributed to all who would receive it, that the presence of such a Gift from God would be held to the utmost of honor and glory? Just how could anything or anyone ever replace such majesty? If it is peace you seek, that name is the One to call upon. If it is power to overcome sin and the flesh, the Almighty God is available at all times, never leaving or forsaking you. If it is need for a father to climb into his lap for counsel, one that was not there for you when you needed him as a child when youthful questions of great importance to you arose, this Father is everlasting and at this very moment is speaking to you aloud in your heart, telling you that He knows what you have need of before you ask.

Speaking to yourself in a way that causes the God of the entire universe to come to you and own the things that you offer unto

Him. Psalms and hymns are written to be harmonized and sung with the promise that is associated with them. Spiritual songs and making melody in your heart is to lay aside the asking part and only turn the page for the One who the words of your heart are directed toward. What has been missing from the relationship that you assumed you owned but really, honestly, rarely, if ever, knew for sure that He was right there all along and you did not leave the place of your meeting unfulfilled and bankrupt of joy because it was not a feeling you were seeking but that presence you knew that came with the personal relationship with the Lord.

David wrote the psalms we enjoy singing and reading because of his gifting from God which would be expressed in a way that kings and noble men would be scorned for doing. Are you a man or woman who cannot prostrate yourself before the Lord in such a way that you believe to be humiliating or at best unlike the person you have portrayed to the ones who know you most intimately? This is not meant to be a condemnation or judgmental question. Our express purpose of this book is to bring about the completion of our relationship with Jesus, the Father, and the Holy Spirit while we have personal time away from the things of day-to-day life and are able to pour our hearts out in ways that touch and hold fast the person of God.

Galatians chapter 4:6 and the verses preceding, tell us this important truth: But when the fulness of the time was come, God sent forth His Son, made of a woman, made under the law, to redeem them that were under the law, that we might receive the adoption of sons. *And because ye are sons, God hath sent forth the Spirit of His Son into your hearts, crying, Abba, Father.*

Crying out, singing, simply speaking in your own hearts what God has placed in them for the moments you feel most need to give back to Him the things that He provides to have perfect relationship while alone in your mind with God. I hope that you are beginning to see the reality of what must have been the heart of the Father while seeking Adam and Eve in the garden. That recollection of Genesis I just inserted into the picture was to give a fresh understanding of what was intended from the foundation of the world to be the most natural meeting between the Creator and His creation while here on earth. That ended because of us. The intention of God was for man to never have to say the words of repentance but only to sing songs of praise and worship to the One who made all things that the Father proclaimed to be good as he rested on that last day of creation. In the world we live in today, it is for certain that expression of self is not something that is lacking both individually or among the masses.

It would be wonderful to say that these expressions were intended to bring about the good of man and to cause a sort of connectivity to take place that would product a positive outcome. For many years, decades and even close to a century, the word peace and equality has been the subject matter of those who feel something is missing. So, millions strive for peace and the need to be heard while it is apparent that something is missing. I believe that what is now being presented to you, the reader, on the idea of a peaceful relationship with each other and those that seek to draw you into a place of acceptance of truths that are contrary to the word of God, these truths are quite the opposite of what is given to us as a standard of living, that being biblical in nature.

I grew up in the sixties as a teenager and young man. I was without a relationship with God at that time and it was not until I was thirty-two years of age that I heard the call of repentance and accepted Jesus Christ as my personal savior. I realize that many of you are unfamiliar with that thinking and that to believe in a God that is not seen is to be without education and knowledge that fits into the comfortable society that is now known to man as one of godlessness; no belief of a higher power and certainly not One that created all of this. Many songs were written and sung in those days that protested the war, or parental thinking or authority. Most became very popular and when drugs and sex entered into the fray, what was offered became the trend of the day. Like the adage, shoot up and drop out, many found that was the way to have relationship with others of like mind and they talked of peace and love as if it were something they had just discovered.

So, the songs that were sung and the ideas of life were put into words of guidance into a place of lifestyle with no god to bother you. You were and are god! Today, we are much more sophisticated and wiser in our own eyes. Spirituality is rampant and embossed into the fabric of daily living. Because of the spirit world reality now, any type of lifestyle that is acceptable to society as a whole. One way to get the attention of a neighbor or fellow worker is to profess and then actually live a life of faith in Jesus Christ. Songs of praise to the Lord and then to lift your hands and offer thanksgiving is to identify with the reality of believing that you can talk to God and He will talk back to you. In that, I believe the narrator would have you know that something may be missing in your relationship because of the society you are a part of without knowing it and without recognizing the fact of the matter, many who would want to be close to and embrace the God of their heart, simply have no idea how to separate from the Monday morning after the Sunday spiritual high, so to speak. This is why we must be those who recognize the deceit all around us and become even more intimate with Jesus and that would mean to find what is missing because you are not alone in this awareness.

David did it right. He knew who he was and acted out his heart for God by singing and praising and worshipping while he was petitioning and asking God for help from the attacks of his enemies but he was in fact on his knees and on his face and in the lap of Abba Father because he found that what was missing in his own life was honesty and humility with his creator. Lord, the world is all around me and I am engulfed with the thinking of it but now I only want to be in Your presence and feel You, smell You, touch You and embrace You to know that I am Yours and You are mine. Write a song to your Savior or to the One who soon will know that you are repentant of your sins. We all have a need to have nearness to the Lord. Do this as your personal love letter to Him. When the room is quiet and the alone part becomes somewhat overwhelming at times because of the feeling of loss, sing your song and praise and honor the One who promises to never leave you. That being done, speak the word of God into your own heart where it will be written not on tables but on the stone of your heart. Songs have a lasting memory about them. You know why one song brings you to tears and another causes you be smile. God would not have written into his eternal word something that was not meant to bring emotion to your life. Our next couple of chapters will take on identity and more action to be taken. For now, love the Lord with songs that are born from the heart of a child while sitting in His lap. Would the people at the office or those next door, understand you for what you are now seeing as the most important person you have chosen to be? Does it matter to you what they would think if they knew about this? Maybe God has a little more work to do in your life that still could be missing something.

CHAPTER 3

I SING OUT A LOVE SONG TO JESUS

FROM THE FIRST MOMENT of realizing there was something missing from a time that I had specifically carved out to be in prayer and devotion to our Lord while reading the bible and hoping to hear His voice of comfort that night, I also knew I was not alone. It wasn't at all noticeable that the thing missing was of grave importance to continue my evening schedule of seeking the heart of God. You know that you have been called to a place of quiet and somewhat seclusion when the sound of silence resonates in your ear. Expectation of excitement or exaltation of what is before you would really be almost unwanted because of the feelings that are there, especially if you approach the hour with a kind of heaviness or even sadness because of the events of the day soon coming to an end.

It is then that the understanding of Who it is you will be spending time with is most wanted and desired so as to place yourself at the mercy of a God who knows all and certainly hears all. Many of you have been walking with the Lord for a great period of time, measured in growth and maturity in Him even more than actual years. Time seems to have a way of reflecting back to us, not in those years, but with memories and very personal snippets of the most unexpected touches that are revealed to us from the unseen. Upon realizing that you are precious and loved more than you can ever be in an earthly way, these new times, as they are and were on these nights give special credence to the word love. Yes, all of us need it sometimes with skin on but in that way, knowing that a person is always available to contact and share the moment that is now upon you, would you say it is given in the same way that it is now in this private place and moment alone with your Savior and Lord?

The apostle John, the author of the gospel, the book of Revelation of Jesus Christ, and the first, second, and third books of John, had a relationship with Jesus for at least three years while Jesus had gathered a group of men together to walk with Him on this earth prior to His crucifixion and death on the cross at calvary. John is often referred to as the apostle of love because he pressed into the person of Jesus and in doing so, many times it is noted that he acted as if he were a favorite of the Lord. Does God have favorites and does He disclose private personal understanding about Himself to those who would press in? Certainly! The phrase used by the other apostles, "the disciple that Jesus loved", was proved out at the last moments of the earthly life of Jesus when He called down from the cross to John that he was to care for Mary, His mother, from that time on. But it must be told at this point in our time together, John knew what love truly meant and where it is found. In First John chapter 4:7-8 he wrote being inspired by the Holy Spirit, "Beloved, let us love one another: for love is of God; and everyone that loveth is born of God, and knowth God. He that loveth not knowth not God; *for God is love.*

Jesus, of course, being God, was love. Of all of ever walked on the face of this earth, He walked completely and totally in love. Jesus understood the meaning of love because of who He is and now to love one another is a command that cannot be rescinded or taken back for any reason. Therefore, dear reader, we must know that for whatever purpose we approach the throne of God and why we desire fellowship with Him is to demonstrate the command that He gave. We do all things to bring our love to Him and that is primary in our relationship. To only come in need for something and to be in expectation of an answer to our request and make that the evidence of our being one with Him is to be missing that something that we are now uncovering and bringing to the forefront of this disclosure.

If what we just received as a reproof or reprimand, thinking that we have been corrected in our desire to honor God, we feel a twinge of self-doubt about the purpose of having those times with the Lord, then the Holy Spirit just visited you and allowed transformation to occur. Well, you say, that is easy to you to write but I am now wondering even more if I truly know the God who I say I trust and believe in. The apostles that were not at the foot of the cross with John and the mother of Jesus, were absent for a good reason. It maybe was not a good reason but to them it was very real. Fear and doubt as to who the man they lived with for over three years and why He is now on a cross dying while He was supposed to be the Son of God and all powerful and did hundreds of miracles and taught and preached the kingdom of God, is leaving us to ourselves without a clear answer to this whole thing. Psalm 68 has a portion of David's heart and the reason why he calls upon the Lord in song so often. That reason is a promise from God before the song is ever sung. The song of praise is about what will take place in the future without understanding the unseen that is only known by the Lord Himself, yet David knew that what he was writing had prophetic words to the reader as this will indicate to you the reader as you see in the next few verses.

> But God shall wound the head of His enemies, and the hairy scalp of such a one as goeth on still in his trespasses. The Lord said, I will bring again from Bashan, *I will bring My people again from the depths of the sea: That thy foot may be dipped in the blood of thine enemies, and the tongue of thy dogs in the same.* They have seen thy goings, O God; even the goings of my God, my King, in the sanctuary. *The singers went before,* the players on instruments followed after; among them were the damsels playing with timbrels.

What is being said here is that it is God who does the work, who sees the needs, and has given the victory while providing solace to the one who would, by faith, enter into communion with the Almighty and all-knowing God. To sing the love song to God, Jesus, the Father, and the Holy Spirit, before speaking one request to them, we, like David, reflect on the majesty of Him and the comfort of His presence, long before we ask or seek a thing. What could be missing from the times of fellowship with the Lord would be answered in the forementioned psalm, the singers went before... Anything that you or I might consider more important than the person of Jesus, the Father, or the Holy Spirit and we have then left the room or wherever we sought to relate to God without what we really needed most.

Love is the key to what is being shared here, dear reader. I am and neither is the narrator, suggesting that you do not know the meaning just because of the idea that missing the Comforter in the time most needed hour is quite possible, and you feel that to be true. When did the singers cry out to the Lord? Where was it that they saw Him? Yes, in the sanctuary. The Hebrew word is translated as set apart or holy. We are never to believe that love is a word that will describe our condition of relationship with Jesus without being set apart. Remember, He is God, who is love and to be in Christ Jesus, then we are to be set apart and cognizant of the fact that to approach the throne of grace is to know that love is my first prerequisite in my ability to enter in.

In conclusion, to finish this section of the manuscript properly and with clear understanding of the topic, reach out for this one thing that you can own personally and with no need to concern yourself again about it. Everything that we will ever have that is given from God will be done for the purpose of glorification of Him the entire time we are on this earth. To simply look at prayer, reading of the word of God, doing works and being obedient to Him will not necessarily show love to Him. Often times the things associated with the Spirit of God become the god themselves. We are warned about the condition of being high minded or thinking more highly of ourselves than we ought. This is exactly why the praise of man and the scripture about the taking place in the temple, illustrates for us the true heart of man towards God in his heavenly realm. Read here found in the gospel of Luke chapter 18:13 and surrounding verses.

> Two men went up into the temple to pray; the one a pharisee, and the other a publican. The pharisee stood and prayed thus with himself, God, I thank Thee, that I am not as other men are, extortioners, unjust, adulterers, or even as this publican. I fast twice in the week; I give tithes of all that I possess. *And the publican, standing afar off, would not lift up so much as his eyes unto heaven, but smote upon his breast, saying, God be merciful to me a sinner.* I tell you; this man went down to his house justified rather than the other: for every one that exalteth himself shall be abased; and he that humbleth himself shall be exalted.

Alone in the place you find to be that which is one of fellowship with the Lord, and to expand that idea of seeking Him at any time that you feel His presence or need to be far from the world and its enticements; dear reader and to myself as your author, we identify with one of these, do we not? To be abased by the Lord would be the most horrifying experience you would ever know. On the other hand, to be exalted would to feel nothing. Exaltation of self is never sought and never known by the humble. But Jesus, here, said that the man would go into his house from the temple and be exalted.

Can I sing out a love song to Jesus and know that I am one who is truly a sinner and that His mercy is so great that I know why I can ask for that mercy? Several acts of the one who is considered a chosen man or woman of God, tell us that we deserve nothing from God but will certainly want and accept every available blessing that he can give at that moment.

So, like David, sing your song. What does that look like to a person who is quiet or better yet, loud and boastful. Many people who attend concerts or sporting events know that when they melt into the group, cheering and booing will be a part of their experience. Absolutely no problem to express oneself when you paid the price of admission and are a follower of the team or entertainer you came to see. How about Jesus? Where does He fit into the life of someone who loves Him but maybe has a hard time with outward praise. Something is missing that would not be missing at the event you paid to get into. How do I express my love for the Savior of my soul and One who willingly came as a baby to grow into a man to die? Death on the cross, exclusively for you and me and really the whole world. The whole world rejected the Gift of the Father and as the gospel of John states they loved and do love darkness more than the light. I think that from now on, at least a love song to Jesus will be the evidence of who you really are and what is happening when you reach out to Him. That personal relationship is going to grow and become the most precious thing that the two of you will ever know.

CHAPTER 4

I LIFT UP MY HANDS

YOU AND I HAVE watched many movies and television programs that begin with titles such as those that contain scenes depicting maybe in a dark alley or an unsuspecting location where just being in the wrong place can create sudden reactions that we are not supposed to even think of doing. Yet, at the moment the sound of the startling voice reaches the ear, it happens. No hesitation, no explanation needed and certainly no instruction is given; the hands go up! What did we just witness? With no warning, the actor surrenders. His or her character is portraying a time when the person committing the robbery or the law enforcement officer surprises the criminal and, in either case, with a pistol in clear sight, the criminal shouts, "I give up, don't shoot" or the robbery victim cries, "don't kill me; take anything you want."

Complete surrender and willful obedience without any questions asked; in both cases, before the assailant or officer said a word. The hands went into the air to signify an understanding of what was expected and then came the instruction from the one holding the pistol. Give me all your money spoken from the thief or you are under arrest from the police officer. This may be an example of something that is far from what this book is all about, but one that strikes a chord if you place yourself in either case.

Analyzing the situation to the event taking place, it really is pretty self-explanatory that there was supposed to be an immediate reaction to the meeting of the two parties. Their relationship in that alley or wherever they would come in contact with each other, tells us that under any other normal circumstance, no one would have thought anything of a casual contact. Actors are often given rolls that demand a very believable performance. In the two examples presented to you as a reader of such unexpected drama, it would not be difficult to put yourself in the place of the character on the screen and imagine what you would do in that situation; one that most likely had never taken place to you in real life or if you had, it truly brought back a few memories.

This is going to be up to our narrator to continue this line of thinking because if we are to transfer the obvious emotion from the temporal to the eternal, He would have to bring into the scene a much more useful and impacting reason to have our attention shifted to that which is not seen. It is not hard to understand the purpose of the beginning of this chapter. The title of it being I lift up my hands. Now, you know, dear reader that you play a part in this book and you also have a responsibility to the author to play your part so that the very benefit of making quality time and a place to receive the answer to the question will be achieved and then become forever engrained into your mind. When the song was sung by you in adoration and praise to Jesus after receiving the answer in the last chapter, a newness of person began to sort of overwhelm you, did it not? I suppose that by doing so, possibly using your own song written specifically to the Lord from your heart, your reaction to the presence of our Savior being that close and with amazing intimacy, you may have gone to your knees or on your face. That would be evidence of the Holy Spirit moving into the time you set aside and He began to show you that what may have been missing from many such times, changed because of the unseen. As the hands went up immediately with no warning of the events that took place in the movie or television show, that song you gave to the Lord in prayer drew you nearer than ever before. This is the most wonderful experience and happening that a believer can have; one orchestrated and certainly not planned; without the flesh becoming the, oh so often one, that makes it impersonal and unfulfilling.

This is now a time to stop the reading and sit back or find a place other than the one you are in presently; away from the familiar and simply, wait. HIS pageturner, the title given to this book, should cause you as the reader to have been attracted to it because it is not so obvious as to what the title is referring to. If you have found your place to wait and listen to the voice of God, it could be that silence would be your companion for a very long period of time. That is actually perfection of your relationship being enhanced and brought into focus. You return when you might feel the calling of the Lord to read on; not before.

> "I am called to live in perfect relationship to God so that my life produces a longing after God in other lives, not admiration for myself. Thoughts about myself hinder my usefulness to God. God is not after perfecting me to be a specimen in his show-room; He is getting me to the place where He can use me. Let Him do what He likes." Oswald Chambers, *My Utmost for His Highest*

Quotes like these from sources of great clarity and purpose help to bring the reason for this book to be written for you and me. The "HIS" in the title is a pronoun specifically placed in the beginning and in capital letters to show the reader that what is given next is to play the part of one who partners with the Most High. It is to be in relationship and harmony with the One we worship and lift our hands up to as a spontaneous act of total surrender to His name, that we understand why we are back to the place we came to communicate with our God. So is pageturner, purposely spelled out in lower case letters, there at the end, to identify something that most of us would confess having never considered the word before, to be a word needing further explanation? It certainly did for me when spoken clearly that night while sitting alone in the dark, near the fireplace, but missing totally the presence of my friend who was taken away from me that afternoon, lifeless, by a total stranger, to be cremated and ashes spread in an area that I would never visit. Don't you know that anyone who would read this sort of mysterious kind of writing, would ask themselves about the times they, themselves have known such emotion and feelings? Then, if the answer is yes, with emphasis on almost uncontrollable emotion to the event, is it okay to be here and in a state of great need? You have come back to this place after going into a silent, undisturbed environment with a listening ear and heart toward the God you love. You knew when the author suggested that to be an interlude from his book that, being inspired by the Holy Spirit, you would find a reason to return and read on. The author was not talking to you then, the narrator was and you understood that an awakening to the Spirit and the missing something was to soon unfold and become newness of life. No doubts or confusion was ever a concern.

Knowing that the pronoun had no other reference other than that of the person of God Himself in the fullness of His being, Father, Son, and Holy Spirit, you have become even more than one who came to ask. Is the word pageturner one that brought you to the place of purchasing or obtaining this book? It certainly would have caused that wanting and interest in me, your author. When it was revealed to me that night, at first, I had no clue as to what the Holy Spirit was asking of me. I had never in my entire life of seventy-seven years, even heard the word or considered what it could mean to me and possibly thousands of others. The time of coming downstairs to my chair alone, had not changed. By that, I mean, reading the proverbs for that day while singing and praising the Lord, although with a heavy heart, I found what I came for. I had no intention of asking Him for any assignments or dreams for that night's sleep. How does it happen to us; those who want to have that closeness to Him but are not sure what to really expect? How did I know that it was to be a special evening of immense revelation and clarity of mind, knowing that I was weak in my person both physically and mentally because of the day's event? To interject a point here that needs to be brought to the forefront; there are going to be times in all of our lives when the desire or want may seem of lesser degree. The subject is our meeting with the Lord, in the place and even time, when it is undisturbed and the quietest and hopefully silent; options to the method of fellowship can vary but the idea, of course, is to establish the very best, solely for the listening to the One we are there to meet.

The pageturner is a term of great passion and intimacy. What I was told to write was meant to reach the heart of the potential bride of Christ, the Lord's wife! Does that surprise you? We know that the "HIS" part of the title, refers to the One we came to meet. That One is known to many of you, myself, and several of those who may never read this book or any literature referring to who we are there for. God is not a casual entity of everyday life. He is One that is brought into our hearts on purpose. You have heard it said many times that He is a perfect gentleman and that to invade a person without permission would be to commit spiritual molestation. It does not mean that He is a God who does not care. The cross of calvary speaks to that issue and makes it clear that the whole world had sinned and needed a Savior. Someone who would be willing to die there and suffer and be separated from the Father in heaven so as to become sin itself to forever pay that price needed for redemption of your soul, and mine, and all of creation past, present, and future. "HIS" is the most wonderful pronoun we can speak of here and now. The title of the book has another part to it and if you are someone who believes that what I just spoke to you and you invited the Holy Spirit into your heart and as the gospel of John speaks clearly, as Jesus told Nicodemus that night, verily, verily, I say unto you, you must to born again.

If you were to close this book right now and go to a bible, King James Version, original text, you would read in the gospel of John chapter three those words. So, without the prompting of the Holy Spirit, you would not now continue to read on. You would abandon the idea of that command from Jesus as being foolish and unacceptable to you because you are more educated and intelligent to buy into sure a concept. Well, it may do you some good to read into the third chapter of John about the dialogue between Jesus and the man who would come to question Him, Nicodemus. He was intelligent and educated but troubled because he knew that his own life did not match up to the thought of being spiritually awakened. You see, dear reader, that is why there is no respect of person with the Lord. Unfortunately, many people in our society around the world use that adage as one that signifies and separates them from the simple words of our Lord. To never seek the Lord with such questions such as the one that Nicodemus was asking and going on into life with only degrees and education, it is completely impossible to see Jesus and ultimately the kingdom of God. Man has made himself . . . god!

The pageturner retreats into the arms of his Creator. What is his purpose of coming, what is your purpose of coming? In conclusion with hands lifted high and songs being sung while finding the answer to the question, the unseen becomes real and the presence of our God is all around. You and I will begin to do a new thing. The reason we will come is not to obtain or ask, although we are commanded to ask anything in the name of Jesus; but to turn the pages and reveal the requests and take our prayers to Him is to be in partnership with the One who ultimately does the work. We are found to be those who realize that all things are possible with the Lord and we then simply enjoy the fellowship and contact in every way by surrender to His majesty. Hands lifted high; songs sung from a grateful heart as we open ourselves up to Him with an action of going from one page to the next. Are you ready to take the position of a lower sort? Lower because of the surrender you now are pleased to have done but never without the fact that you have been given an assignment tied solely to the King of Kings and now you stand on the wall as a watchman of the king with no desire to be inside the box. God is greater than any box and to then be so closely related in such a personal relationship is overwhelming and again the hands immediately go up!

CHAPTER 5

I LIFT UP MY HANDS TO THE LORD

MOST OF YOU HAVE a pretty good idea as to who and what the name of Jesus conveys. I also know that if you were to be asked about the name given to Jesus you might refer to Him as Lord. When asked about who God is we often state the fact of the Trinity which is to say, He, God, is one but with three persons, all equal but with totally different names, purposes and tasks. We will not be getting too deeply into hermeneutics or numerology but we probably should look into the names that are listed in the table of contents.

The song that we sing in our congregations that has now become the starting point of this book, refers to and states that Jesus is Yeshua, our Savior and Redeemer, and that being Lord, Kurois, is Master of all and then, not stated but understood, finally God Himself, Elohim, Theos, all powerful and almighty, all knowing and all present. It is then taken for granted that God is there, omnipresent, whenever we use the words, Jesus, Lord, Spirit, Father and so many more that describe who we sing and lift our hands up to worship. Chapter 4 cleared the way to what is now to be one that will offer to the reader an even more intimate insight as to who we are personally related to.

We realize that the song, using the name of Jesus and then changing it to Lord when exercising a different action when using our voices and heartfelt outpouring and then to look up with our hands stretched out to heaven, signaling that we believe in an unseen deity who is seated at the right hand of the Father but not just there; He is nearer than we would ever have imagined He would be, with us and in us! Please take note. We are all individuals with needs and wants that no one else has exactly like ours. But, as we individually possess characteristics of mankind, we are not as of mankind at all. Each man or woman's individuality will prove out to be a curse or a blessing when the moment comes, like *in moments like these*!

When, then, can individuality become a curse to us? The exact moment that you and I are called into the presence of God; that time when we are lost in our sin and cannot break the barriers of it to see what is needed to become whole, our individuality rises up and promotes itself. You might find yourself saying, "I will not do that thing to cause me to believe that an unseen God is calling me to a place of relationship with Him". That thing is possibly the only answer to why we lack personality. Mr. Author, what are you talking about? This is a book that is supposed to help me find the answer to what is missing; that something that is preventing me from really knowing the Lord and feeling His presence. Ok, Mr. or Miss reader, being the pageturner that is to understand your relationship in the fellowship you desire to have with God, Jesus, the Lord, you must have a personality that allows you to know that He is omnipresent, not by education or knowledge alone but by one thing. If you were Nicodemus and had this burning desire to know more than what you have seen in Him, you then lay down your individuality and embrace personality; you and the Lord. You are not just sitting in your chair, as I was that night, but we now find that we are drawn there and that our only hope is to partner with the Master, the Lord and we acknowledge that with immediate song, hands lifted, embraces and closeness before we even bring forth our requests or reading of the word, we commune. We simply talk to Him, sit quietly, and when He is ready, we surrender ourselves to begin to turn pages that He knows about and has known about since the beginning of time.

Does that make sense? Before Nicodemus asked the question, Jesus told him that he must be born again. Of the spirit of God, the wonderful counselor, who knows everything we will ever need to know. Jesus, our Lord, leaving this earth and not returning until His Father instructs Him to do so again, which may be very soon, says to us that He has to go so that the comforter will come. He will be greater than Jesus Himself and we will do greater things than Jesus did! What are we being told here by our wonderful counselor, our narrator? It is the Lord! Who is the Lord who we are lifting hands to? Kurios; Master of all. I sing out a love song to Jesus and I lift up my hands to Him, my Master! Is He? Is He Lord of all in your life? I want to be HIS pageturner, which I had no idea what the Holy Spirit was telling me to become.

In the 1973 movie version of *Godspell*, Robin says "Master", day by day, day by day, oh dear Lord three things I pray; to see Thee more clearly, love Thee more dearly, follow Thee more nearly, day by day. Then Jesus puts up one finger and she puts her one finger on His and repeats the three things with an additional finger coming from Jesus until three are up and they are touching each other and then begins the joyful dancing and celebrating the work of Jesus.

The movie is loaded with interaction with Jesus and those who would follow Him and do His will. The Master was there with them at all times and with His instruction they became HIS pageturner(s). The relationship between God and all those who would desire to be with Him became evident to all who could see with their hearts and spiritual eyes opened wide, the meetings were spontaneous and real with no false humility or on the other side of the spectrum, pride.

Exactly what is the reason that a new understand of our relationship with Jesus is so important to the Holy Spirit, our narrator?

I am only a man who for these last several years of my life, began to see that God wants to have more than service to Him. Many of us have been called to do things throughout our lifetime as believers. The idea we should have been, isn't that we work for God but that we are so loyal to Him that He can work through us. God wants to use us as He used His own Son. Now we are beginning to see that who God is and who we are is not something that is capable of being separated. Once the Holy Spirit is born into our heart and resides in what is commonly referred to as the temple, we are then not our own. There exists a loyalty to Jesus far beyond the comprehension of the mind of man. To position one's self in a state of loyalty is to surrender the will of that person to that of God. Remember when we were introduced to the concept of individuality earlier? To prevent the individual from gaining personality with the Lord would be to become one who would never be loyal and useable to and for the Almighty. A scripture that will help in your journey to the place of the pageturner is found in the book of Acts chapter 1:8; when here Jesus said, "you will be My witnesses." He meant *witnesses who satisfy Me in any circumstance I put you in, witnesses I am counting on for extreme service, with no complaining on your part and no explanation on Mine.*

Is this the kind of God you expected to have as you found yourself walking in the flesh, not to commit outright sin, but to do service for the Lord!? He has told us that we are to be witnesses in any form of service He requires with no complaining and then no explanation of why He is calling upon you to be that witness. I would say that it will take someone that is so loyal and so mindful of His presence and closeness, that to turn the page for God is to know we are one with Him. Remember Kairos, Lord, denotes the overpowering and yet kind and just God that is truly master. When can a master with the ability to create and then destroy that creation if He wills, ever be just in the hearts and minds of ones who will place our entire trust in Him?

In the wonderful series of books written by C.S. Lewis, one stands out as probably the most famous, that being the *Lion, the Witch and the Wardrobe*. The characters and the humanized animals and creatures found while in Narnia, often had conversation about things that brought great spiritual truth to light. As humorous as is sounds, there is nothing funny about this one.

> *"Is—is he a man?" asked Lucy.*
>
> *"Aslan a man!" said Mr. Beaver sternly. "Certainly not. I tell you he is the king of the wood and the son of the great emperor-beyond-the-sea. Don't you know who is the king of beasts? Aslan is a lion—the lion, the great lion."*
>
> *"Ooh!" said Susan, "I'd thought he was a man. Is he—quite safe? I shall feel rather nervous about meeting a lion."*
>
> *"That you will, dearie, and no mistake," said Mrs. Beaver; "if there's anyone who can appear before Aslan without their knees knocking, they're either braver than most or else just silly."*
>
> *"Then he isn't safe?" said Lucy.*
>
> *"Safe?" said Mr. Beaver; "don't you hear what Mrs. Beaver tells you? Who said anything about safe? 'Course he isn't safe. But he's good. He's the king, I tell you."*

When you hear or read that while watching the video or reading the book, a certain kind of wonderment comes over you if you are capturing the meaning of the questions and answers that are given. It would seem that to go on would be taking a huge chance in facing such a one that is so powerful. In that, dear reader lies the very reasons of going on in this manuscript. You are not done yet with the missing something! Well, I know what you are going to reveal next Mr. Author, and I also know what is missing from the moments like those I would experience in Hs presence. Okay, tell me, without looking further into this chapter or those yet to come. You have spoken to yourself the completed source of information needed to finish the book for all of us to read. That is fine and if that is what you are looking for and maybe found it, then like the children in the Narnia series, do not go on and meet Aslan; turn back and enter into the wardrobe and into the world that you came from without ever getting to stand face to face with a lion!? You can reply if you wish. The lion is not what we are talking about, are we? The something that I feel is missing, you might reply back to this author and then the narrator, should look like more of a lamb, after all didn't Jesus take on the characteristics of a lamb that was slain? Yes, exactly as a lamb that was slain. But, because of the thought that we can be sure of the character of our master, that being as a slain lamb, would it be foolish of us to think that He is that way now? The book of Revelation chapter five covers the entire issue in a canopy of truth and eternal quizzical statements that appear to be contradictory in natural.

And one of the elders saith unto me, weep not: behold, the lion of the tribe of Judah, the root of David, hath prevailed to open the book, and to loosen the seven seals thereof. And I beheld, and, lo, in the midst of the throne and of the four beasts, and in the midst of the elders, stood a Lamb as it had been slain, having seven horns and seven eyes, which are the seven spirits of God sent forth into all the earth. Kind of a mystery here; but not really. When referring to God, remember, He has many names and many functions and many characteristics that differ when the occasion arises and it does often. It does make perfect sense to see Jesus as the Lamb and at the same time the Lion.

Lifting up our hands is certainly a direct sign of praise but also something that results in the loyalty we spoke of earlier. My hands and yours allow us to do tasks and designed by our creator to be useful in so many ways. Could it be that a more useful way to present them would be as one that shows our willingness to God to, in fact, turn pages of life and obedience when we are called into this presence. After all, it is not the flesh that seeks the relationship we have with Jesus. We do so because of the Holy Spirit wanting and desiring us to be in fellowship in moments like these.

CHAPTER 6

SINGING I LOVE YOU, LORD (3)

THE TITLE OF THIS chapter written here above might bring to your memory the things we saw in chapter 3. In comparison to the love song that was sung to the Lord Jesus, this is quite different in that it really is not a song at all in this chapter 6. Look closely to the wording that is included in the entire song we sing in the congregation. Not only that but this time we have in triplicate, the most intimate words that can be spoken to Jesus. They are the same as the ones we say to our spouses or family members, maybe even to someone who we have known for a long period of time as a friend, who is more than an acquaintance but not in our inner circle; one who is special and worthy of our highest admiration. Does singing have to include or exclude a song? Is it the song that is to be exalted and placed in the archives of man as those that place the Lord in the highest place or can it be simply a noise?

What is the Holy Spirit attempting to say to us about addressing the Lord and when is it joyful and accepted by Him? This entire chapter could be dedicated solely to the number of times that expression of joy and singing is spoken of in scripture. I will leave that up to you. What may be of some interest to you about the words that appear in the title of this chapter is interpretation. Because we came into this time of being pageturner(s) and not just casual participants with the Lord a few times each day, there has been discovered quite by chance, seemingly, but of course, all orchestrated by the Holy Spirit, we now have to investigate a new clue to our missing something. Chapter three describes an action that is happening as we offer up to Jesus a song of love; a love song. This chapter is one of singing that same song but doing so with repetition and with love as the central theme of that action. Does any of this mean to you, my fellow worshipper and intimate friend of our Lord, that we have become those who have free expression of love?

It is important at this stage of our understanding that we have knowledge of words that often are interchanged, mostly by the world and used in fleshly ways, that can and will further our eternal relationship with God. One such word that magnifies the person of Jesus is agape. This love is not an earthly type of emotion but one of complete unselfishness and unconditional in everything that is associated with it. Other forms of love, such as eros, being romantic; that of the flesh and sexual in nature is not used when describing our intimacy with our Lord. *Phileo* is a brotherly love that is experienced in a deep friendship. *Storge* is one that involves the family and is shared with parents toward children and siblings. *Xenia* can be shown in many ways but mostly in hospitality and generosity with strangers and guests. One more is *Pragma*, which is explained as a love that will endure with longevity and commitment amongst those in association even in times of great challenge. *Philuatia* is love of self but not in a way that is in opposition of the word of God but actually is expressed and commanded by Jesus as the second greatest commandment of all. In the gospel of Matthew chapter 22 he says *Thou shalt love the Lord thy God with all thy heart, and with all thy soul, and with all thy mind. This is the first and great commandment. And the second is like unto it, thou shalt love thy neighbor as thyself. On these two commandments hang all the law and the prophets.* Simple definitions of the word love but not at all simple in the use of them. The only one we have to look intently at in moments like these is that of *Agape*. It is a Greek word found often in the New Testament and is always associated with *God!* No mistake should ever be made in describing *Agape* because in the small epistle written by the apostle John being his First in chapter 4:7-8 *Beloved, let us love one another: for love is of God; and every one that loveth is born of God, and knoweth God. He that loveth not knoweth not God; for God is love.* Getting right to the point of our chapter title, singing I love you, Lord, we have an incredible mention of truth that can only cause us to *sing*, bursting out with unrestrained, selfless and unguarded emotion proclaiming His word to be true.

Let us now settle back into our place of solitude or if it is one that came about in a spontaneous fashion, maybe not as private but yet supplied by our narrator, the Holy Spirit; we gather our thoughts. If something had truly been missing, by our own admission, of some sort of dissatisfaction in numerous times of meeting the Lord but seldom having a born-again experience, that being filled with and having the joy come upon us, can we assign to it some sort of cure? You have thought many things over up until this point, haven't you? HIS pageturner, describing what the Holy Spirit is calling us, has taken on a new and, frankly, very welcome moniker of who and what I am and you are also and most likely have been since Jesus came into our hearts; we being the temples of his Holy Spirit.

So why the new title or explanation as to who and what we are to Him? We will let the narrator of this piece of work take the stage of which he is entitled to as we clear it for Him in our hearts and minds. After all, it could be just so that what has been the trouble with what has been missing is solely because we did not see Him as such. The action word here is *see!*

We open our Bibles, take out our journals, spread out our prayer materials that have been accumulated for decades. Our devotionals are worn and so familiar and we approach this time with anticipation of having that which we call intimacy with God to be one of the unseen. This could not be a temporal meeting of common worldly procedures. Business meetings and work-related issues, family gatherings and coffee with a friend. No, my Savior, please not just one more of those. I do come prepared but if it only is more of the familiar and really kind of a duty that so many years of church activities and meetings with other church leaders have caused me to think that this is what following Jesus means; no, Lord, not this time I beg and beseech you. What was just uttered and seemed to be a crying out for a newness of the relationship needed to know Him not just with our head knowledge but with a heart filled with true love, we have entered into the unseen. All the things that we brought into the devotional time are those that are aids in helping us see the Lord. Opening the word of God is what is needed daily, probably more than daily, to feed us the bread of life that is living in Jesus Himself. Here is where we start the obvious. It is God's word and we are reading it for many reasons but at some time we may have become the example of the church in Ephesus. Most of you are very familiar with the Second chapter of the book of Revelation.

> Unto the angel of the church of Ephesus write; these things saith he that holdeth the seven stars in His right hand, who walketh in the midst of the seven golden candlesticks; I know thy works, and thy labor, and thy patience, and how thou canst not bear them which are evil: and thou hast tried them which say they are apostles, and are not, and hast found them liars: And hast borne, and hast patience, and for My name's sake hast labored, and hast not fainted. Nevertheless, I have somewhat against thee, *because thou hast left thy first love.*

Notice the first three verses of the chapter. There would be no other church, seemingly, that we all should be a part of, such as this one. What then is the problem? Remember, this is the revelation given to the apostle John while exiled on the island of Patmos in the Aegean Sea, by the angel sent from Jesus, in heaven, at the right hand of His Father, as a warning! Church of Ephesus, you have become such a group of believers that the leadership, the pastor, has now started to lead you away from the truth and into works related to God but not with Him at all because you have left your first love, that being Jesus Christ, the Lord and Master of all, Himself. It is not impossible for many of you, while seeking the Lord, to miss Him altogether and leave your space unfulfilled only because of the mistaken doctrine of the church that has told you how to approach God but not to be aware of false instruction. Revelation chapter two alone is enough to alert any serious born-again believer of the doctrines of devils, as spoken of in the book of first Timothy chapter four. Mr. Author, you are now going too far. I am not here to be lectured on the way my church is being led or if I am following false doctrine taught there knowingly or unknowingly.

Dear reader, you are correct in that your author is not here to do that but quite possibly the Holy Spirit is. Please read on into Revelation chapter two below.

> *Remember therefore from whence thou art fallen, and repent, and do the first works; or else I will come unto thee quickly, and will remove thy candlestick out of His place, except thou repent. But this thou hast, that thou hatest the deeds of the Nicolaitans, which I also hate. He that hath an ear, let him hear what the Spirit saith unto the churches; to him that overcometh will I give to eat of the tree of life, which is in the midst of the paradise of God.*

Again, please note, that the warning is to the church, the pastor, and anyone who has an ear to hear what the Spirit saith. These are very hard words to incorporate into the mind and heart of one who has believed that he or she has been walking faithfully with the Lord and therefore is on the path of righteousness and would never have expected to be told that all that is being done while having left your first love, Jesus! This is the very reason the Holy Spirit has instructed the author to prevent those, who want the fullness of the Lord, to continue on in desperation and be so unfulfilled that you begin to question if you know Him at all. The love between the Lord Jesus and His bride, which is the remnant of the church that are doers of the word and not hearers only, is evident in the book of Revelation chapters two and three. The very last book and the last written word from Jesus' mouth to anyone, was to seven churches that existed during the time of the early church.

Only two of the churches did not receive rebuke. Can you understand that it only took less than fifty to sixty years for the Christian faith to begin to deteriorate and follow another gospel, but believe that they were doing the same as Jesus did while on earth!? How much more do we all need to examine our faith and motives to be able to sing, I love you, lord?

With two chapters left in this book to bring conclusion to the reader any doubts of relationship with God, please take a lot of time and searching of heart to correctly place yourself in the group that is without rebuke or correction from Jesus. We will reveal more of what our narrator has in mind to cleanse the soul of sin and guilt. Here is the thing, it all is for the purification of the reader who now has been made aware of the missing something. Love is going to be a word from now on that is only spoken to the Most High from a heart filled with overflowing thanksgiving and eyes set upon the cross of calvary where God nailed His Son to die in our place. The question still stands, in moments like these, the ones that you just heard from a God of love; is your first love still the only true love of your life?

— *CHAPTER 7* —

I LOVE YOU

SHE POSSESSED ONE OF the most beautiful voices ever to sing a song. She won numerous awards for acting, music, and comedy. In 1991 she performed a song that got her nominated for the grammy award that year. Somewhat of a protest song, it talks about man and his place that he occupies while on earth but with a message of hope and love because "from a distance" God is watching us and that should give comfort to anyone who is feeling the stress and anger toward war and guns. Bette Midler certainly had fame that brought her into contact with so many people who would listen intently for her messages of complete foolishness and falsehoods! There you go again, Mr. Author, why is it that you have to write such unkind criticism. It is a well-known fact that "from a distance" is a song recorded by many artists because of the beautiful words of hope and kindness of man's hearts toward one another in spite of the ugliness of war and the use of guns. Also, to bring God into the picture of his awareness of the state of mankind, he is always present . . . from a distance. As a matter of fact, he is watching us, as the lyrics point out. What more could be said that would convince you, our author of this book, to possibly correct your thoughts of Ms. Midler being wrong in her presentation of the song. Is it not true that God is watching us from a distance?

Okay, I could have asked the narrator about these comments that I made prior to giving my thoughts on the matter. But, if you have been reading this from the beginning, you would already understand that any and all of this manuscript is the work of the Holy Spirit. Examples of the scriptures are scattered throughout the eight chapters; the word of God is spoken even without those references and most of the time, I am sure that you would agree, that you, the reader, have yourselves been moved and touched by the words on these pages. So, let me start over with this thought coming now from our God, the Holy Spirit. The title of this chapter is I love you; that being the last line in the love song posted in the table of contents. In chapter six, singing I love you, Lord, repeated three times to emphasize the expression of love we are to have for the Lord, love is the central action word given because God is love, as we saw in the first epistle of John. It is not because I have not been listening to the narrator as to the presentation of instruction and manner of subject before, I place one letter of the alphabet on the page, it is because of that very thing that the song by Bette Midler was brought to my attention. Singing a song, especially in the one mentioned titled, from a distance, has got to carry an emotion of the heart to reach the hearer and then for that hearer to file it away in their mind. I was sure that you had done that with the words in the title of chapter six, as unto the Lord. The point is made that now we have a song that is not unto the Lord but does bring Him into the picture of the mind of the hearer. Is it possible that could happen to you, the reader, when you sing a love song to Jesus, our Lord? It has been brought to your attention in other places in this book, that singing does not just include the song. The expression of love in the title of the sixth chapter is directed at the Lord.

In this next to the last chapter of HIS pageturner, you have to conclude your reading with a, for sure, reason to have an expectation of finding or correcting the subject matter that caused you to pick up this book. If something was missing and you were not aware of it until the Holy Spirit, our wonderful counselor, touched your heart with a need for more from Him, by now it is clearer to you what you were feeling and not just feeling but knowing and wanting all that is available through the love of God. I love you! Remember back when we were shown that love is a very used and misused word in the language that we are speaking today. Those seven known words, with translations into the usage that is presented to the one spoken to, are meant to bring personality to our relationships. So, it is quite apparent to all of us, that the One we are directing our attention to in this book is one of the persons in the Holy Trinity; or if we are truly engaged with our worship and prayers, we have choices to speak, as the song is sung, to the Lord, or Jesus, or Father, or our narrator, the Holy Spirit, or Yahweh, Elohim, Adonai, names of God in Hebrew.

I point this out from a distance, that being away for the statements I made about foolishness and falsehood, aware or unaware, is necessary to uncover truth.! Does telling God, you agape Hm sound like a nearness to Him or a distance? Why not a lifting of your hands to the Lord and praising Him with the word Emmanuel? Does that sound like God is watching us from a distance? To really get this off the ground, so to speak, how about a very silent, soft spoken, three words of pure selflessness, without it being directed at any of the Three; just a simple "I love you", as the end of our song resonates from our emptied heart.

It takes sometimes years for a new believer to find what can be missing for so long. Because, dear reader, you are still searching and seeking the magnificence of God, while all the while you knew that you wanted so much more. You know who you are and confess that and repent often for any transgressions that seem to overwhelm you. Closeness and nearness to Jesus is asked from your lips to have Him draw you into Himself only to experience the lack of that very thing. This being the place in time that God has chosen for you, man or woman, young person or older, healthy in body or in suffering, owning and possessing much of this world's goods or living a life that, without explanation, with using the talents you thought were enough, you failed time and again; when the holidays and parties came around, you were invited to places that joy and good cheer abounded or the apartment over the drug store has been your best friend most of your adult life, where the telephone never rings unless it is a wrong number.

Is this the God that is watching from a distance? No, he is not watching from a distance but is nearer to you, HIS pagerturner, because I, your author, just removed the space between the capital s and the lower-case p. You and God could not be any closer than that, at least not while on earth. I would like the privilege of being Linus in the Charlie Brown Christmas. He told the story of all stories of the first coming of Jesus from heaven to become man on this earth. Jesus understands apartments over drug stores and careers that were overshadowed by that of your sister or brother. He came into his world, born of a mere human woman and that happening in a cave with animals and their waste all around. You may not be able to change your circumstances and neither could Jesus but when you are acting as HIS pageturner, in whatever capacity that is asked of you by the King born in a manger in Bethlehem, He is not any distance away from you and you are there next to Him as Robin sang in *Godspell*, to follow thee more nearly, day by day.

In and because of your love for Jesus, the Father in heaven, very near to His Son, being at His right hand, is about to make your relationship become inseparable. My story is one of Jesus being sent back again. His Father has a present for Him. In the days of Jesus, a wedding was a very big deal. If it were a Galilean wedding, it was even more of all of that. To bring the betrothed man and woman together was to bring the whole village of Galileans together. Witnesses of what was to take place next. It was all centered around the cup! It was offered by the soon to be groom to his bride to be as an invitation to solidify their coming union. She could back out, refuse taking the cup, and everyone would go their way but if she took and drank of the cup, that signified that she wanted him for her spouse, her bridegroom. A dowry was given and they separated then to begin the process of preparation for the wedding itself.

What is most important to see from this acceptance of the cup by the bride to be is that once that covenant is formed between herself and the groom to be, then the time before the wedding will take place is one that is solely for preparation. Can you say that when you received the Holy Spirit into your heart as an act of betrothal to God, you knew that one day there would be a wedding in heaven and a feast to celebrate that event? All the things that have been shared up to this point in the book are about our relationship with the Lord on earth. But, to know that this relationship is really much more than church activity and doing good works and reading the word of God and seeking to obey and love God, would be the answer to something that could be missing. You, dear pageturner, have been spending years, day by day, possibly, attempting to reach the Lord, thinking that He was only from a distance, even though, with knowledge and understanding, to be born again is to have Him living inside you; you being the temple of the Holy Spirit. All this time, it is exactly like the preparation in a Galilean wedding. You are His wife to be and with that said, it is you that made the covenant possible, agreeing to have Jesus as your bridegroom. He has never been closer than He was the day you accepted Him and He then began His preparation to bring you into His Father's house. Cast aside any thoughts of earning your way into His heart. Never again see yourself as unworthy and damaged goods when you are, yourself making preparations with purification and garments spotless and only waiting for one thing; the Father in heaven to send His Son to rescue you from the world that has never been your home. Finally, in the gospel of John, chapter fourteen, the deal is sealed and the words of Jesus seals it for all time.

> Let not your heart be troubled: ye believe in God, believe also in Me. In My Father's house are many mansions: if it were not so, I would have told you. *I go to prepare a place for you. And if I go and prepare a place for you, I will come again, and receive you unto Myself; that where I am, there ye may be also.* And whither I go ye know, and the way ye know. Thomas saith unto Him, Lord, we know not whither thou goest; and how can we know the way? Jesus saith unto him, I am the Way, the Truth, and the Life: no man cometh unto the Father, but by Me.

My dear beloved saint; our narrator, the Holy Spirit, gave this word to you for the comfort and enjoyment of knowing that your position of *HIS pageturner* is to assure you that when the place that you choose to meet Him, where or when that is to be, will be one of partnership, just as in the wedding. Those prayers of intercession, that opening of His word, the devotionals and journals that you include in your daily worship and praise to your soon to be groom, He has always been near to you from the inside of your heart. Therefore, in moments like these, it will be for you to know that what is on your heart when coming to a special place or one that is convenient for the moment, you will turn the pages as He directs you to do but never will he consider you as only HIS pageturner, which is of a higher calling but not for long. That night when the doors of the Father's house are closed and locked and the feast begins inside, nothing on the outside again will matter but only that which is happening between you and your Bridegroom. Something will then be missing; lies, pain, hurt, loneliness, and sin. So, for now, we sing a love song to the Lord, lift up our hands and rejoice in the fact that, as we look to the cross of our Savior, you are kneeling there looking up into His face and knowing that even though you sing of love to Him, He first loved and does still love you for all eternity. Amen

CHAPTER 8

NEW LOVE—NEW BEGINNINGS

Often when a revelation is given and the content of that revelation is made clear, or clearer than it had been previously, we sit back and look at the thing that was now made new and think about it. When we are quite sure that it will be something that is going to change the way, we consider that matter, we forget about it and go on with our daily lives as if nothing really did metamorphosize. That way of seeing things change and the reaction to them can become a habit that will alter the entire scope of our lives. Up until now, our Holy Spirit has given truly a revelation that could renew the hearts and minds of us all, not only in the temporal world we are a part of but more importantly, that one of the unseen; eternity. You have read the first seven chapters of this book knowing that something had been missing from our times with Jesus and now have been given a clarity which supplied us with the knowledge of being HIS pageturner. HIS pageturner with so much more feeling and understanding that we are His chosen for a purpose. That purpose is to be with Him and to exercise the gifts that are ours only because of the personal relationship we enjoy and embrace. When we go into times of prayer and intercession, praise and worship with songs of love and hands lifted up to the One we are pressed into, there is no wonderment of His presence any longer but the assurance of what will be when the most intimate of the touch will feel like. Of course, He is with you at all times and you are His temple, but when He calls you to Himself and you respond in that way only you and He can know, nothing can replace that and nothing ever will!

> 2 Kings Chapter 6:2-7
>
> Let us go, we pray thee, unto Jordan, and take thence every man a beam, and let us make us a place there, where we may dwell. And he answered, Go ye. And one said, be content, I pray thee, and go with thy servants. And he answered, I will go. So, he went with them. And when they came to Jordan, they cut down wood. *But as one was felling a beam, the axe head fell into the water: and he cried, and said, alas, master! for it was borrowed. And the man of God said, where fell it? And he shewed him the place. And he cut down a stick, and cast it in thither; and the iron did swim. Therefore, said he, Take it up to thee. And he put out his hand, and took it. Then the king of Syria warred against Israel, and took counsel with his servants, saying, in such and such a place shall be my camp.*

Mr. Author, I feel that you are trying to get me to read a section of the Old Testament because you have the Book of Second Kings on your mind now but how does that fit into those things you just wrote? I confess that if our narrator, the Holy Spirit had not confided in me about the direction for the conclusion of this manuscript, I would not have blamed you for asking that question. He wants to make a life changing moment like this, to prevent us from ever loosing that which we learned in the Second Chapter of the Book of Revelation of Jesus Christ. I will leave that reading up to you but without a doubt this passage of scripture tells a story of immense importance to the remnant of the church who desires to become the eternal bride of Christ. Those Corinthians did not know it at the time but when the letter was given to John on the island of Patmos and then passed on to the pastor of that church in Ephesus, all of the truth about the axe head and the stick would come together like adhesive material. If the love of Jesus was the topic of the letter sent to that group of unsuspecting believers who thought that they were free of the sin of Corinth because of their ways of following God, then what does Second Kings show us? Reading the text, it appears that the actions of the men to cross over the Jordan River into a land that they desired to dwell in, set up a home, a place for families and work to ensure future living of their children and now an event takes place that is recorded. This man of God, the prophet Elisha, was told by a man with servants, that the beams that were to be cut down would be somewhat of a problem. That problem was the implement to down the trees was gone and had fallen into the river water. The axe head sank into the depths of the water and it appeared to halt the work that had to be done. Not only that but the one who lost the axe head made of iron, had borrowed it and now he could not retrieve it. Elisha, a man of great faith and having heard the voice and calling of the Lord God was told by the man that it was lost.

The letter from the angel to John sent from heaven by Jesus, told a very incriminating story. Nevertheless, I have somewhat against thee, because thou hast *left thy first love.* So now, in the book of Second Kings, Elisha is the man of God, cried out to be the one who has come to do a good work but carelessly, used the axe and lost the iron head, rendering the tool, useless. We learned in previous chapters of this book, many names of God. One was the same as what Elisha was referred to by the man, master. Does that ring out to you? Master, in a time of great need and with no one else around to help this man's dilemma, the man of God is called upon. Master, even lord, small letter l, because he was not God but one who was known for his life of divine service to Elohim. Where did you lose the axe head? In another way to say the same thing to the Corinthians, when did you leave your first love? I lost the axe somewhere around here. How do you recover an object that is gone and is really heavy and with no way to reach it? How do you recover a love that is only found in Jesus once you leave it, knowingly or otherwise.

Elisha, with the power given him by God, shows how that iron object will be found. He throws in a stick around the area where the man thought he may have lost it. Amazingly and to all that would be watching this, the axe head floats to the surface and is plucked up and renewed to the handle. What was believed to be worthless because the iron was gone, became new again and useful to the man who had borrowed it. What was the object lesson of the story preserved for all time? Jesus, the first love of all who come to Him for salvation, can many times be left behind as the cares of the world bring us to places where leaving Him is not even thought to be that because we are doing the work. Like the stick that was applied to the situation of the lost implement, so too is the Cross of Jesus, to cause us to see what has often times been missing because we have really left that love, Jesus Himself. The axe head swims, floats to the surface and is recovered, made new. The believer is graciously rebuked by Jesus and thoroughly explains to the unaware or purposeful follower, that the Holy Spirit will be taken away forever unless he looks up to the Cross of Jesus and repents with a heart of sorrow, and then be renewed, made. again.

Our title of this chapter is highlighted by the word New. It was pointed out in a previous chapter that numerology and hermeneutics would play a part in HIS pageturner. I was, as your author, given a tap on the shoulder by the Holy Spirit and also a mandate that came from a source to continue on into the book with chapter eight. As so many of you are also students of the Word and those things related to understanding aspects of it, you have learned about numerology and found it to be so amazing that the inspired Word of God contains so many examples of biblical teachings of the subject. So, to see the number eight is to know that it represents the term of new beginnings. One reason almost all of you will know is the events leading up to the great flood. So many truths are found in that one remarkable story which happened with the renewal of the inhabitants and everything related to the earth. But mankind was the primary recipient of the wrath of God when the entire population of the world was swallowed up and then drowned leaving a rather large vessel afloat on the top of the waters with a set of new inhabitants and thousands of animal species and every living thing, Specifically, God would reward Noah and his three sons and their wives with the saving of them from what the disaster of sorts, caused. The grand total of mankind was eight! Thus, we have the second part of our title NEW BEGINNINGS. What is really something that should never be forgotten as the ultimate in a new beginning is the resurrection of Jesus Christ, our wonderful Lord and Savior, Emmanuel. When on the eighth day, He rose victorious and bringing with Him new life for all who would believe and truth in His Holy Name; be born again of His Spirit and live life on the new earth in fellowship with Him. Praise, worship, thanksgiving, honor, glory, devotion and love, now and forever, unto the King of kings and Lord of lords.

We have investigated the words for God, for love, and our title of this book. What we need to know now to continue on into the place that the finish line is visible; is new is a word that can be defined in numerous ways? So, let's say that the opposite of this word would almost in the majority to defined as old. But sorry to say, that is not in the realm of what is to be disclosed as our word new. With the near completion of the manuscript before the Holy Spirit breathed upon it and enlarged the number of pages and words, His spoke of a NEW LOVE. I looked high and low, researched the idea of new love, specifically, in biblical terms; inspired. Nothing! Prayer is a way of finding the heart of God. What do you want the reader to know now after he or she has discovered what may have been missing and how they relate to Jesus as HIS pageturner? Is love something that could be defined as a new thing? The Holy Spirit certainly does think and most definitely knows that it can be and should be. Okay, then, all the time we spent in the words and meaning of the word love is there for our understanding, but no new love.

We are left with the word *new*. I will tell you now that I have never considered what the Holy Spirit wants us all to know, no, not one time in my entire seventy-seven years of life on this planet. But, I will, say, as I attempt to enlighten you all with the new way to look at love, it was always there but not completely spelled out as such. New is fresh after an event. New is recently produced by change. New is renovate, repair so as to recover the first state! I did not make this up to show that the scriptures that the Holy Spirit gave in Second Kings and Revelation chapter two would mesh into what I probably know that is apparent to all of you. Back in the beginning; the introduction of this book, was a passage of scripture you may want to turn to now. Don't do that, I will show it here. 2 Timothy Chapter 3:16

> *All scripture is given by inspiration of God, and is profitable for doctrine, for reproof, for correction, for instruction in righteousness: That the man of God may be perfect, thoroughly furnished unto all good works.*

Inspiration of God. Then the words man of God. Finally, perfect. The reason for the God we serve to speak to us is that we may be perfect; we being the man of God. I only hope that this very finite author is bringing understanding to you, the dear reader, man of God, to a place of perfection. Now look at this word, furnished! New is to renovate. New is fresh and produced by change, recently. In moments like these. He is not watching from a distance. Jesus is here! Can we sin when we are at the communion table of the Lord? Pressing into His side, the one that was pierced with a sword but out came water and blood. He became man so that we could become those who know Him intimately and like Robin in *Godspell* called out to Him. "Master. Day by day, day by day, oh dear Lord three things I pray, to see thee more clearly, love thee more dearly, follow then more nearly, day by day. Is that you?"

Fresh love and a changed heart and mind. So, what does this all mean practically? Believe my dear saint, this part of the new love, new beginnings hit hard because of the years I have lived, with and without the salvation of Jesus Christ. If you happen to be one that has taken the time to read all of this and yet, yet, you are saying to yourself that what is described here is not what I have been living. Some will even confess that this brand of religion is not what I signed up for. Why so much spiritual rhetoric and jargon? Okay, where does that leave you? Yes, I was captivated by the book title but now it is more than that. I really do not want to spend my life in such a way that I give up everything that defines me. Relationship with God Himself? Isn't going to church once in a while and being good person the real way to get to heaven, if there is such a place? If you have asked that question, you are not alone. But, HIS pageturner is not about religion. Not even about going to church. Certainly not about good works, although those will come because of a love for the Savior, not to be seen of men. So, this author mentioned practical living. One that probably will require this newness of life and love.

> *The second greatest commandment of all. In the gospel of Matthew chapter 22 he says*
>
> *Thou shalt love the Lord thy God with all thy heart, and with all thy soul, and with all thy mind.*
>
> *This is the first and great commandment.*
>
> *And the second is like unto it, thou shalt love thy neighbor as thyself.*
>
> *On these two commandments hang all the law and the prophets.*

What would you define the opposite of love to be now that you know all the different meanings of love from our previous chapters? Could it be that while your everyday life is being lived out in all the normal ways that we do, that as individuals and groups, families and coworkers, neighbors and sometime acquaintances, friends, those who are not friends but we know, even intimately, love is not the word we would use to describe our feeling with any of them. You may have answered the question with a resounding, hate or even hatred. The research I did find was that synonyms for the word hate are more than you would imagine.

Despise, scorn, grudge, antagonism, antipathy, odium, maliciousness, aversion, invidiousness, spitefulness, horror, rancor, pique, vitriol, virulence, venom, jaundice, spleen, cattiness, disdain loathing, abhorrence, detestation, disgust, jealous, hostility, execration, resentment, malice bitterness, hatefulness, malevolence, meanness, revulsion, animosity, spitefulness, repulsion malignancy, malignity, repugnance, enmity.

I am sure that I cannot give a specific definition for these words, let alone pronounce them, but I can say that as I found them being the opposite of the love, we have spent hours discussing, they seem to have a way of breaking up the party, so to speak. Why did our narrator, the wonderful, guide to our lives, our Holy Spirit, bring this to our attention? Just as we have been given great insight to our relationship with Jesus and will continue to do so all the more as we seek to praise and worship Him; it is imperative that a truth be known about the other side of our being. Does the new term HIS pageturner have anything to do with that side of all of us? Of course it does. To separate the character of man and not still have body, soul, and spirit alive would be to put to death the flesh not in a spiritual way but in a physical, fleshly way; bodily death. But we are not dead. When is death a welcome event in any of our lives? When I had my friend and constant companion, Paulie, our yellow labrador retriever put to sleep that day, I did not welcome that task at hand but did know that for him it would be a release of the pain and suffering he was experiencing. So, now what about all those words for hate or hatred. The world we now live in is remarkable in the sense that expressions of anger and open vulgarity now are part of every aspect of society. There is no such thing as a worldly love that is being cried out for. That was a very hard sentence to write. Peace, joy, happiness, contentment, respect, and all the other sought-after things that would heal this planet from where we are now, seem to be just words. I am still with the plan that the Holy Spirit intends to make clear. Sin, of course, is not something that can be ignored and to do just that would be to say that this book and the greatest of all books, the Word of God, is either one that is perfectly fine with God to have it now published with hundreds of additions and subtractions, along with changing of the word altogether and gender equal with the word God completely removed as our standard. We are obliged to be those who's standard is constant and never changing when we look into His Word. Going back or looking back into the chapters that have love as the main theme and to see the word in this chapter being that of new, it is obvious that the world we are a part of and contribute to on a daily basis needs to have HIS pageturner to remind them of what change should look like. Did any of those words related to hate cause you to stop and think about a relationship or one that at one time was more in line with what would be pleasing to Jesus?

New is fresh after an event. New is recently produced by change. New is renovate, repair so as to recover the first state! I do believe that the axe head that was lost for a period of time seen in the book of Second Kings could be our subject toward the path that leads to the final word from our narrator. What good is a handle without the axe head? Also, what would it be like to have no solution to the lose? In the book of Revelation of Jesus Christ, the rebuke was not concerning the loss of Jesus but it was the leaving of Jesus, our first love. Either way, it is imperative that we be the ones that seek to remedy the situation. You did that with the understanding of your nearness and partnership in obeying the call to be HIS pageturner in all aspects of life, spiritually and now fleshly. Mr. Author, please get to the point of what the Holy Spirit is about to reveal. I am thankful, dear reader, for your attention and input as we near the end.

We are one in this next assignment and there will be a test, and more tests. There will be homework unlike any you have ever had before, most assuredly, you will have to apply what you have learned in the first seven chapters and now begin to search your hearts for the courage and fortitude to continue on.

All of us have people in our lives that are not easily loved! Several may be easier to, using one of those words, dislike. The most difficult of all is to admit to self that the ones you are related to by blood can be the most difficult to be around. I want to start with the spouses. In my own marriage of almost fifty-seven years, there were many times when that union appeared to be headed for disaster. I do not want to spend time talking about me because this is not about me. Children have been raised in Godly homes, that term is used a lot, but not correctly. In homes that Jesus is Lord and Savior but the atmosphere is one that does not reflect that at all. So, an adult child leaves the home and does not communicate with the parents or follow the Lord; none of us want that to ever be the case but all too often it is just that. What is the solution to put the words new beginnings into the picture? It is that NEW LOVE that is available to those who would humble themselves and at least pray for a FRESH, CHANGE, TO RENOVATE, REPAIR so as to recover the first state. The hands go up and the song is sung where before despair and anguish resided. Who could have ever believed that the understanding of who we are before the great and mighty Healer, Jehovah Rapha, being HIS pageturner could bring about a miraculous change in our families, not to mention the lesser of relationships we have with those in our neighborhoods, towns and cities, states and countries.

Dear precious reader, we have One who is here, not there. He is present, not distant or afar. Alive and aware of your troubles and joys, trials and victories, and mine also. Let us now take the last of moments like these to enter in to the throne room of God in prayer and thanksgiving.

Heavenly Father, Almighty and merciful Lord, Son of the Most High, Creator and maintainer of the universe. We thank You for the Holy Spirit that has given us this text and illustration of who You really are. If we can ask for one thing it would be to know You more and serve You more. We look up and yearn for Your soon return, to be one with You for all eternity, leaving the temporal for the eternal, the seen for the unseen, but one day face to face. Glory be unto Your name, that name above all names, JESUS. Amen.

www.ingramcontent.com/pod-product-compliance
Lightning Source LLC
Chambersburg PA
CBHW061512040426
42450CB00008B/1573

* 9 7 9 8 3 8 5 2 4 5 9 0 1 *